THE AWESOME BOOK OF

WORLD OF WOW WONDER

PLANETS
AND THEIR MOONS

Get ready to hear your kids say, "Wow! That's awesome!" as they dive into this fun, informative, question-answering series of books! Students—and teachers and parents—will learn things about the world around them that they never knew before!

This approach to education seeks to promote an interest in learning by answering questions kids have always wondered about. When books answer questions that kids already want to know the answers to, kids love to read those books, fostering a love for reading and learning, the true keys to lifelong education.

Colorful graphics are labeled and explained to connect with visual learners, while entertaining explanations of each subject will connect with those who prefer reading or listening as their learning style.

This educational series makes learning fun through many levels of interaction. The in-depth information combined with fantastic illustrations promote learning and retention, while question and answer boxes reinforce the subject matter to promote higher order thinking.

Teachers and parents love this series because it engages young people, sparking an interest and desire in learning. It doesn't feel like work to learn about a new subject with books this interactive and interesting.

This set of books will be an addition to your home or classroom library that everyone will enjoy. And, before you know it, you too will be saying, "Wow! That's awesome!"

"People cannot learn by having information pressed into their brains. Knowledge has to be sucked into the brain, not pushed in. First, one must create a state of mind that craves knowledge, interest, and wonder. You can teach only by creating an urge to know." - Victor Weisskopf

© 2014 Flowerpot Press

Contents under license from Aladdin Books Ltd.

Flowerpot Press
142 2nd Avenue North
Franklin, TN 37064

Flowerpot Press is a Division of Kamalu LLC, Franklin, TN, U.S.A. and Flowerpot Children's Press, Inc., Oakville, ON, Canada.

ISBN 978-1-4867-0342-5

Written by:
John Farndon

Illustrators:
Ian Thompson
Mike Saunders
Peter Kesteven
Jo Moore

American Edition Editor:
Johannah Gilman Paiva

Designer:
David West
Children's Books

American Redesign:
Jonas Fearon Bell

Copy Editor:
Kimberly Horg

Educational Consultant:
Jim Heacock

Printed in China.

CONTENTS

INTRODUCTION

Have you ever wondered what lies in space beyond the comfort of our planet? There is a whole family of planets in the Solar System, many with their own moons.

This book will take you out into space, to explore Mercury and Venus, stopping at Earth and our Moon, and then on to Mars, Jupiter, Saturn, Uranus, Neptune, and the dwarf planet Pluto. Discover the amazing moons that orbit these planets, and learn about other features in the Solar System, such as asteroids, comets, and meteoroids.

Can you find?

Q: Why watch out for these boxes?

A: They give answers to the space questions you always wanted to ask!

Zoom in on...

Space Bits
Look out for these boxes to take a closer look at space features.

Awesome Facts
Watch out for these diamonds to learn more truly weird and wonderful facts about space and the universe in which we live.

PLANETS AND THEIR MOONS

The Earth doesn't just hang in space. It zooms at almost 67,000 mph (107,826 km/h) around the Sun. Earth isn't alone. Another seven huge orbs, called "planets," circle the Sun, too—all held in place by the pull of the Sun's gravity. The Sun, its planets and their moons, and comets and asteroids are together called the "Solar System."

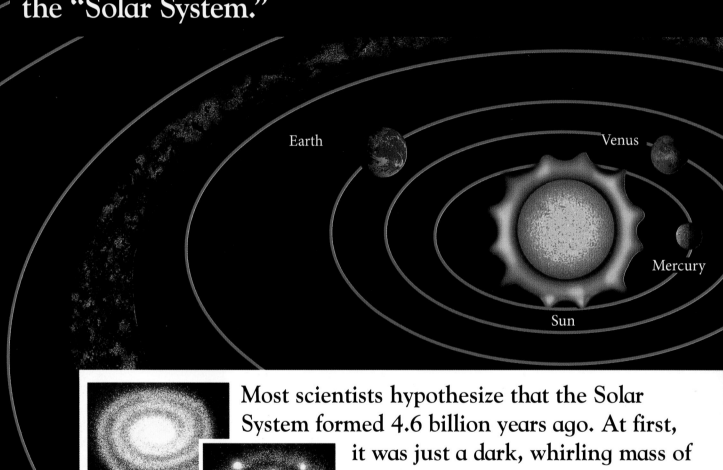

Most scientists hypothesize that the Solar System formed 4.6 billion years ago. At first, it was just a dark, whirling mass of gas and dust. But as it spun, gravity pulled bits tighter together. The dense center became the Sun, and dust farther out came together to form the planets.

The four planets closest to the Sun are Mercury, Venus, Earth, and Mars. They are all quite small and are made mainly of rock. The next four are Jupiter, Saturn, Uranus, and Neptune. They are all gas giants and are made of hydrogen, helium, and other gases.

Neptune

Uranus

Awesome Facts
The Solar System is at least 12 billion miles (19 billion km) across. If Earth were the size of a grain of salt, the Solar System would be as big as a sports stadium.

Mars

Saturn

Asteroid belt

Jupiter

How many planets are in the Solar System?

MERCURY

Mercury is the nearest planet to the Sun, often less than 36 million miles (58 million km) away. Mercury has little atmosphere, so the side facing the Sun can be more than 801°F (427°C), while the dark side is an icy cold -279°F (-173°C).

Earth turns around once on its axis in 24 hours (in relation to the Sun). Mercury takes nearly 59 Earth days to turn once around its axis.

Like Earth, Mercury has polar ice caps.

Mercury

About every decade, Mercury passes across the face of the Sun when seen from the Earth. This is called a "transit."

famous writers and composers.

Zoom in on...

Mercury's surface

Earth

Mercury

Mercury is smaller than some of Jupiter's moons. It is 20 times lighter than Earth and barely a third of the diameter.

Q: If Mercury takes nearly 59 days to turn around, why does the Sun stay up for 176 days?

A: Mercury rotates slowly, but whizzes around the Sun in just 88 days (compared to 365 days for Earth). This means that as it turns slowly away from the Sun, it whizzes around the other side, so that the sunny side is still facing the Sun.

Mercury is small, so its gravity is very weak and can't hold onto an atmosphere. There is nothing to protect the planet from the Sun's rays or to stop meteoroids and comets from bashing into it. As a result, it is deeply dented with craters, just like the Moon. A journey across the surface would show you vast, empty basins, cliffs hundreds of miles long, and yellow dust everywhere.

VENUS

Venus is almost exactly the same size as Earth.
It measures about 7,500 miles (12,070 km) across and
weighs just a little less than Earth. It is sometimes
called the "Evening Star" or the "Morning Star."
This is because it is quite close to the Sun, so
it can be seen in the night sky just after sunset
or just before sunrise.

Zoom in on...

Atmosphere

Venus is a
beautiful planet,
covered in swirls
of pinkish-white cloud.
The pink clouds are actually
made partly of sulfuric acid.
They are so thick, they press
down on the planet's surface
hard enough to crush a car!

Venus

Moon

When our Moon is a
new crescent moon, it is
between the Earth and the
Sun. Venus lies between
the Earth and the Sun,
too. So sometimes you
will see Venus near the
new Moon as it rises.

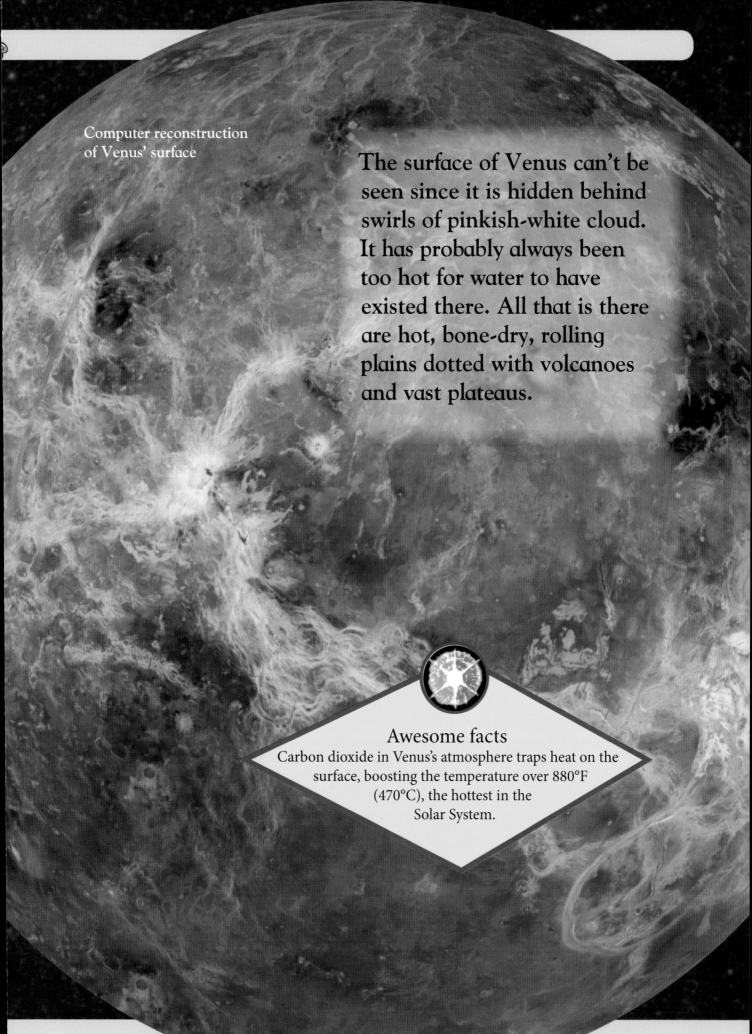

Computer reconstruction
of Venus' surface

The surface of Venus can't be
seen since it is hidden behind
swirls of pinkish-white cloud.
It has probably always been
too hot for water to have
existed there. All that is there
are hot, bone-dry, rolling
plains dotted with volcanoes
and vast plateaus.

Awesome facts

Carbon dioxide in Venus's atmosphere traps heat on the
surface, boosting the temperature over 880°F
(470°C), the hottest in the
Solar System.

PLANET EARTH

Earth is the third planet out from the Sun, about 93 million miles (150 million km) away. It is not so close to the Sun that it is scorching hot, nor so far away that it is icy cold. It has water on its surface, and can sustain life.

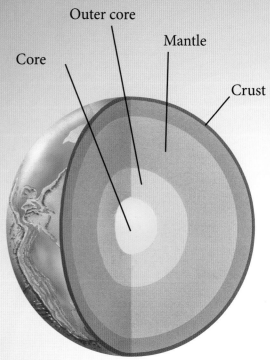

The Earth is made mainly of rock and is the densest planet in the Solar System. But it is not just a solid ball. It has a shell, or crust, of hard rock. Beneath that is a layer about 1,850 miles (2,977 km) deep of warm, partly melted rock, called the "mantle." The center is a core made entirely of hot metal, mostly iron.

Q: Why can we live on our planet?

A: Earth is a special place. It is the only planet that we know has water on its surface, and water makes life possible. It also has a blanket of gases, called the "atmosphere," which we breathe.

Earth is not round!

Earth is not quite round. It bulges at the middle, around the equator. Going through Earth from pole to pole is 27 miles (43 km) shorter than going between opposite points on the equator.

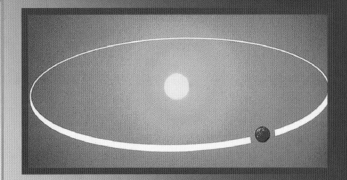

Earth whizzes once around the Sun every year. It is slightly tilted over. So, as it travels around the Sun, the zone on Earth tilted toward the Sun gradually shifts. This is what creates seasons—the part of the world tilted toward the Sun has summer, and the part that is tilted away has winter, so when it is summer in North America, it is winter in Australia. The equator has no seasons.

70% of Earth is ocean. Can you spot the land?

OUR MOON

The Moon is Earth's closest companion. It is about 240,000 miles (386,243 km) away. The Moon circles around Earth about once a month—which is how we got the word "month" (or "moonth").

The Moon seems to change shape over a month. We only see the side of the Moon that is lit by the Sun. As the Moon circles Earth, we see it from different angles—and so see more or less of its sunlit side.

1

The Moon is a barren, lifeless place covered with dust and craters caused by huge meteorites crashing into it billions of years ago.

2

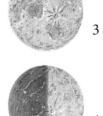
3

At the new moon (1), we see a thin crescent-shaped sliver. This grows over the next two weeks to a full moon (3), when we see all of the sunlit side. It then shrinks back over the rest of the month to a crescent-shape—the old moon (5).

4

5

Q: How was the Moon made?

A: Amazingly, the Moon was probably made by a space collision. Scientists hypothesize that 4.5 billion years ago, soon after the Earth formed, a planet at least as big as Mars collided with Earth. The crash completely melted the other planet, and splashes flew off into space. Gradually, gravity pulled these splashes together into a ball, which cooled to form the Moon.

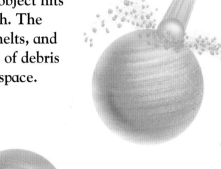

A large object hits the Earth. The object melts, and splashes of debris fly into space.

Debris spins in orbit and joins together to form the Moon.

Surface of the Moon

MARS

Mars is the only planet to have an atmosphere or daytime temperatures anything like ours. But Mars is a desert planet, with no oceans—just red rocks and dust and a pink sky.

Ice-covered pole

 Q: Are there any volcanoes on Mars?

A: Like Earth and Venus, Mars has volcanoes. In fact, Olympus Mons (below) on Mars is the biggest volcano in the Solar System—three times higher than Mount Everest!

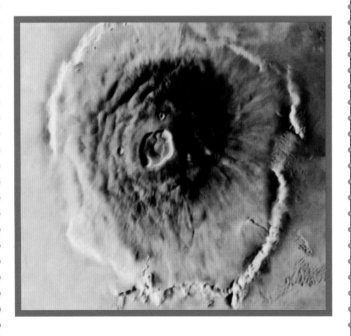

More spacecraft have landed on Mars than on any planet. In 1997, the Mars *Pathfinder* landed and sent out a robot truck to scan the area and beam back TV pictures. In 2012, the *Curiosity* rover landed on Mars for a two-year search for signs of life.

Craters on
Mars' surface

Zoom in on...

Water on Mars?

In the 1880s, astronomers
thought dark lines they saw
on Mars' surface were actually canals
built by Martians. They proved to be
optical illusions, but valleys show that
water once flowed over the surface in
abundance.

ASTEROIDS, COMETS, AND METEOROIDS

There are hundreds of thousands of tiny pieces of rock and ice whizzing around the Sun, including asteroids, comets, and meteoroids. Some are no bigger than raisins, but the biggest asteroid, called "Ceres," is 579 miles (932 km) across. Two asteroids even have their own moons!

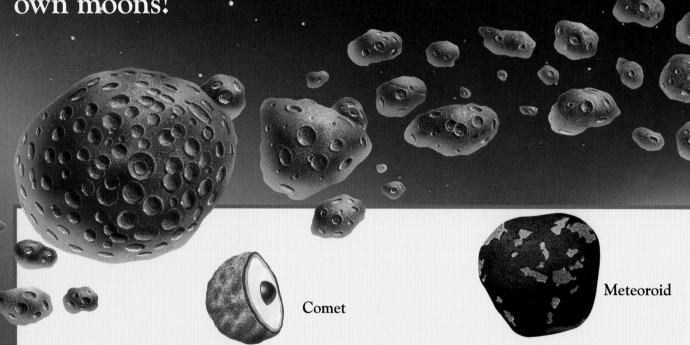

Comet

Meteoroid

A meteoroid is dirt and debris from an asteroid or comet. It can be seen as a meteor as it burns in Earth's atmosphere. If it reaches Earth, it is usually no bigger than a lump of coal, and is called a "meteorite." Comets are like huge, dirty snowballs in the outer reaches of the Solar System. A comet's core can be almost 15 miles (24 km) across, but when it swings in close to the Sun and partly melts, it throws out a vast glistening tail of dust and gas.

Halley's Comet is visible for several weeks every 76 years or so.

The Meteor Crater in Arizona is a vast bowl that formed when a meteorite crashed into the desert an estimated 50,000 years ago. The bowl is 4,000 feet (1,219 m) across and 650 feet (198 m) deep.

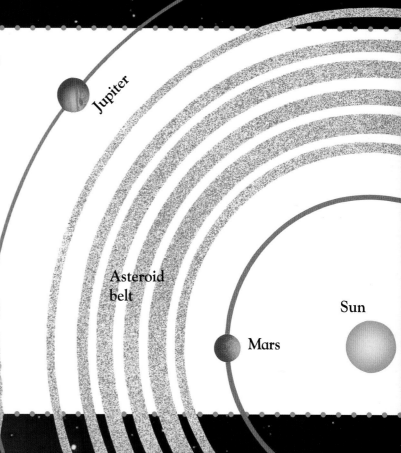

Q: Where are most asteroids found?

A: Most asteroids circle the Sun in a huge band between Mars and Jupiter called the "asteroid belt." It may be the last remnants of a smashed planet. There are 26 asteroids that are over 25 miles (40 km) across, over a million that are just over half a mile (0.8 km) across, and billions of smaller pieces!

Jupiter

Asteroid belt

Sun

Mars

JUPITER

Jupiter is gigantic. It is by far the biggest planet in the Solar System—over 88,000 miles (141,622 km) across—and it takes 12 years to go around the Sun. It is an enormous ball of gas, more like the Sun than like the Earth, and is made mainly of hydrogen and helium. You can see it clearly for part of the year—it is brighter than any of the stars.

Q: What is the red spot?

A: The Great Red Spot, or "GRS," is a dark red swirl of clouds in Jupiter's atmosphere that was first noticed more than 300 years ago. It seems to be a gigantic hurricane, with very strong winds.

Can you find the Great Red Spot?

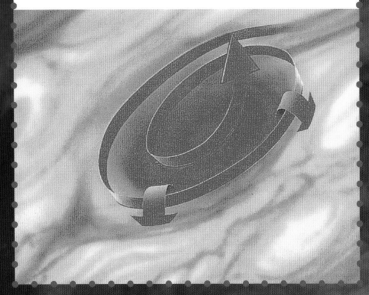

Jupiter weighs 318 times as much as Earth. Its colorful clouds are whipped into long belts by violent winds up to 300 miles per hour (483 km/h).

Jupiter's gravity is so powerful that it squeezes hydrogen and helium gases until they become liquid or solid. Under the thin atmosphere is an ocean of liquid hydrogen and a small rocky core.

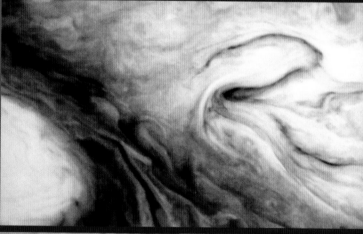

Awesome Facts
Jupiter revolves once in 10 Earth hours, compared to 24 hours for Earth. Jupiter's equator is revolving at 30,000 miles per hour (48,280 km/h)!

JUPITER'S MOONS

Jupiter has at least 16 moons. The four largest (Io, Europa, Ganymede, and Callisto) were discovered by the scientist Galileo Galilei in 1610. Ganymede and Callisto are larger than our own Moon, and the other two are not much smaller.

Until Galileo saw through his telescope that Jupiter's moons circled around it, people thought that everything in the universe circled around our Earth.

Ganymede

Jupiter

If you were on Ganymede, you would see Jupiter in the sky.

Awesome Facts
Jupiter has 16 known moons, but there may be others too small to have been seen yet. You can see the four biggest moons with an ordinary pair of binoculars!

Europa

Callisto

Io

Zoom in on...

Europa's oceans

Europa has a very bright, smooth surface of ice, possibly with liquid water beneath. Scientists think that there might be life forms in this water. In places, the surface of Europa is cracked like an eggshell.

Io has been called the most volcanic body in the Solar System. When the *Voyager 2* space probe passed it in 1979, it discovered that plumes of material were being shot out from Io's surface up to a height of nearly 200 miles (322 km). It was the first evidence of active volcanoes anywhere other than Earth.

SATURN

Saturn is the second largest planet, a gas giant over 74,000 miles (119,091 km) across. Saturn is known as the "Ringed Planet" because around it circles amazing rings stretching out 43,000 miles (69,202 km). Saturn's core is made of rock twice as hot as the Sun's surface.

Q: What are Saturn's rings made of?

A: Saturn's rings are bands of countless billions of tiny blocks of ice and dust, circling the planet endlessly. Each ring is thousands of miles wide.

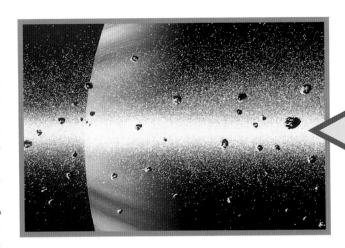

Awesome Facts
When Galileo first discovered Saturn's rings in 1610, he thought the planet had "ears" or "handles" because his telescope wasn't sharp enough.

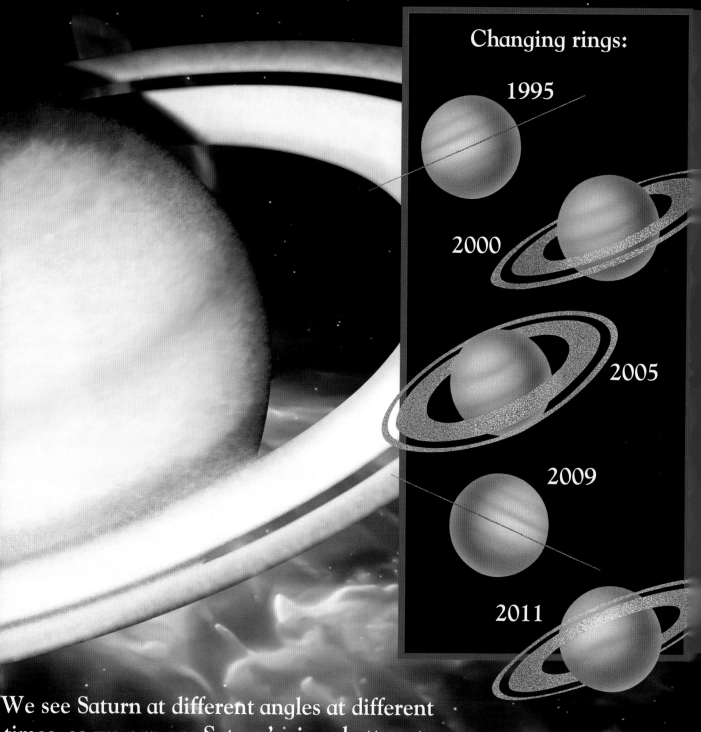

1995

2000

2005

2009

2011

We see Saturn at different angles at different times, so we can see Saturn's rings better at some times than others. In 1995, the rings were edge-on and hard to see. In 2005, they were at a greater angle, which gave us a clear view.

URANUS

Uranus is so far from the Sun that temperatures on its surface drop to -357°F (-216°C). In this amazing cold, the methane (natural gas) that covers the planet turns to liquid oceans thousands of miles deep. It is the methane gas that gives Uranus its beautiful blue color.

Awesome Facts

Because Uranus rolls around the Sun on its side, the Sun does some odd things. In spring, the Sun rises and sets every nine hours—backward.

Uranus tilts so far that it's on its side. It spins around once every 17 hours, but this has no effect on the length of a day. Instead, the day depends on where Uranus is in its orbit. When the south pole is pointing directly at the Sun, the Sun doesn't go down there for 20 years!

Planet spins on its side.

Uranus' icy atmosphere is made of hydrogen and helium. Winds whistle through it at over 1,250 mph (2,012 km/h), ten times faster than the fastest hurricane on Earth. If you fell into its icy oceans for even a fraction of a second, you'd freeze so hard you could be shattered like glass.

Uranus' moon, Oberon

Zoom in on...

Long year

Uranus is almost 2 billion miles (2.9 billion km) from the Sun. It is so far out, the distance Uranus has to travel around the Sun takes more than 84 Earth years. So on Uranus, you would be collecting your pension on your first birthday!

NEPTUNE

Neptune is the fourth-largest planet in the Solar System. It's so far from the Sun— about 2.8 billion miles (4.5 billion km)—that it takes 164.79 years to go around the Sun. Indeed, it hasn't even gone around once since it was first discovered back in 1846.

Awesome Facts

Neptune is the windiest place in the Solar System, with winds of over 1,500 miles per hour (2,414 km/h)—faster than the fastest jet plane.

Cloud features on Neptune's surface.

Zoom in on...

Scooter

Neptune has raging storms and clouds on its surface that come and go over the years, probably driven by Neptune's internal heat. It also has a small white cloud of methane ice crystals that zips around the planet once every 16 hours and so is now known as the Scooter.

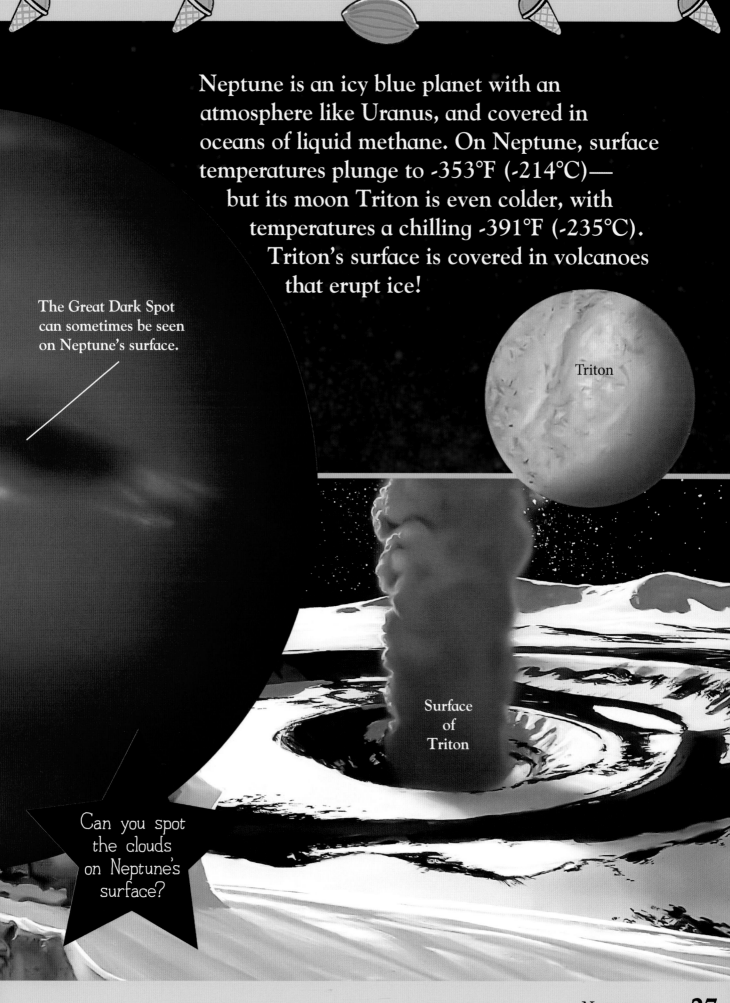

Neptune is an icy blue planet with an atmosphere like Uranus, and covered in oceans of liquid methane. On Neptune, surface temperatures plunge to -353°F (-214°C)— but its moon Triton is even colder, with temperatures a chilling -391°F (-235°C). Triton's surface is covered in volcanoes that erupt ice!

The Great Dark Spot can sometimes be seen on Neptune's surface.

Triton

Surface of Triton

Can you spot the clouds on Neptune's surface?

THE DWARF PLANET PLUTO

Pluto is a dwarf planet in our Solar System—
a tiny, lonely world smaller than our Moon. It is so
far from the Sun, that from Pluto, the Sun looks little
bigger than a star in the sky. Sunlight only takes eight
minutes to reach Earth, but takes up to six hours to
reach Pluto.

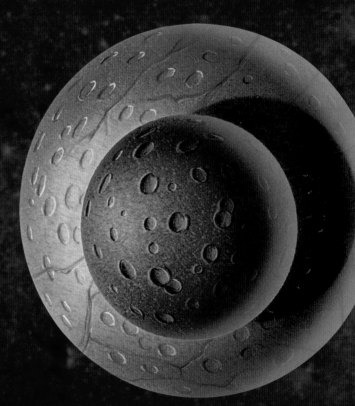

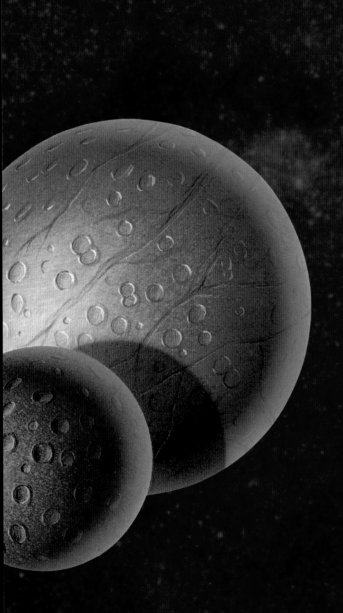

Pluto has a moon almost half its size,
called "Charon." Pluto and Charon
circle around each other, locked
together in space like a weightlifter's
dumbbell. So Charon always stays in th
same place in Pluto's sky, looking eigh
times as big as our Moon.

Zoom in on...

Charlene!

The man who found Charon in 1978 was going to name it after his wife, Charlene. But he chose "Charon" after the ferryman who took lost souls to the Greek underworld, land of Pluto.

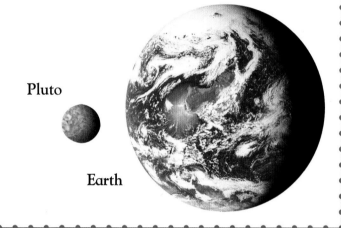

Q: How big is Pluto compared to Earth?

A: Pluto is only 1,432 miles (2,305 km) across, barely a fifth of the size of Earth. Because it is so small and hard to spot, Pluto was not discovered until 1930.

Pluto

Earth

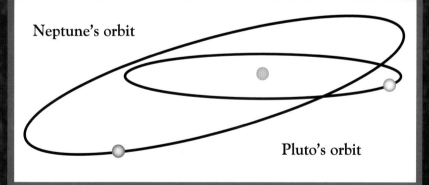

Neptune's orbit

Pluto's orbit

Pluto has an odd, oval orbit. Most of the time, it is billions of miles out beyond Neptune. But for several years every three centuries, it actually moves in closer to the Sun than Neptune.

PLANET FACTS

Use the table below to help you compare some fascinating facts about the eight planets in our Solar System. Use the illustration (below) to remind you of their order.

PLANET	NO. OF MOONs	MASS x EARTH	DISTANCE FROM SUN (MILLIONS OF MILES)	LENGTH OF YEAR
Mercury	0	0.055	36 (58 km)	88 days
Venus	0	0.82	67 (108 km)	225 days
Earth	1	1.00	93 (150 km)	365.25 days
Mars	2	0.11	142 (228 km)	687 days
Jupiter	16	317.8	483 (778 km)	11.9 years
Saturn	22	95.2	886 (1,427 km)	29.5 years
Uranus	15	14.5	1,784 (2,871 km)	84.1 years
Neptune	8	17.2	2,795 (4,498 km)	164.9 years

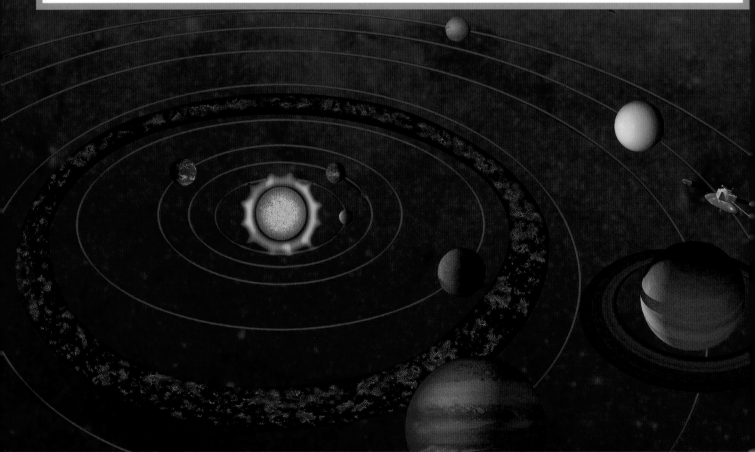

GLOSSARY

Asteroids
Small, rocky objects, the greatest collection of which orbit the Sun in a band called "the asteroid belt," between Mars and Jupiter.

Atmosphere
The layer of gases that surrounds a planet. The atmosphere around Earth supplies us with the oxygen that keeps us alive.

Comets
Lumps of ice and dust that orbit the Sun. As a comet approaches the Sun, heat from the Sun causes the ice and dust to boil off, creating huge tails that stretch out behind the comet.

Crater
A bowl-shaped pit on the surface of a planet. Some are caused by volcanoes, and some by the impact of a meteoroid.

Equator
An imaginary line that runs around the middle of a planet at an equal distance from its two poles.

Gravity
Every object in the universe has a force that attracts it to every other object. This force is called "gravity." The Solar System is held together by the Sun's gravitational pull.

Great Red Spot
A dark red swirl of clouds in Jupiter's atmosphere.

Meteorite
A meteor that hits Earth's surface.

Meteoroids
Small pieces of space debris that orbit the Sun.

Meteors
Objects that hit Earth's atmosphere and burn up, leaving a fiery trail that disappears after a few seconds.

Moons
Small bodies that orbit around some of the major planets. Earth has one moon, while Venus has none, and Jupiter has 16.

Orbit
The path of an object, such as a planet or a comet, around another object, such as a star.

Planets
Large objects that orbit around a star. These can be rocky planets such as Earth, Venus, or Mars, or gassy giant planets, such as Jupiter, Saturn, or Uranus.

Pole
A point on a planet's surface around which the planet spins or rotates.

Solar System
The group of major planets, including Earth, and minor planets that orbit the Sun.

INDEX